Using Essences for Animal Healing

By Georgina Cyr

www.animal-communicator.com
Last Reprint: 2/23/2015

Copyright © Georgina Cyr, 2005

Essences

Essences are liquid "formulas" of the actual **energetic patterns** of a plant, flower, tree, gem, or other natural substance. An Essence will not physically contain any of the actual substance, they simply **resonate** the substance's qualities. They vibrate at a very high energetic frequency that is holographic in nature.

An Essence is a vibrational remedy **generally taken orally**. They help in a subtle **non-invasive way** with **emotional, physical and spiritual well-being**.

Neither an Essential oil nor an Essence is a medicinal herbal preparation.

A Herbal Preparation or Remedy is a substance containing the chemical compositions of a plant and is generally used as a "medicine" for assisting healing of the physical body.

What is the difference between an Essential oil and an Essence?

Essential oils are concentrated plant essences, they are not truly oils at all. They are referred to as oils because of their extreme concentration of the plant oils derived, usually from the process of distillation. They are powerfully concentrated and **one only needs a minute dose**. They are not to be taken internally. They are **for external use only**.

The History of Essences

The first therapeutic essences were the **Bach Flower Essences** created by the British physician Dr. Edward Bach in 1931. He had studied under **Dr. Samuel Hahnemann**, the creator of homeopathic remedies. Dr Bach created 38 flower essences as a complete system of treatment for health.

Dr. Bach's Flower essences remained as the only known flower essences until around the 1970's when Richard Katz and Patricia Kininski produced the **California Flower Essences** and founded the **Flower Essence Society** (FES). **http://www.flowersociety.org/about.htm.**

Essences Today

Canadian Tree Forest Essences, developed by **Daniel Tigner** and **Celine Cloutier** in the 1970's. These essences carry a **deep resonance** of individual and combinations of trees, helping both animals and humans deal with the multiple situations, transitions, difficulties and natural cycles of life. **http://www.essences.ca/**

Sharon Callahan's Anaflora Essences are made with esoteric, spiritual flowers as well as traditional ones. She offers **special blends** that she has created especially for animals as well as **custom blends** which she will create specifically for your animal. **http://www.anaflora.com/index.htm**

Ruth Joy has created essences from the **Angelic Realm**, and also essences made from the vibrations of the **Shamanic Wild Animals** on the planet. She also makes Indigo essences and offers an Indigo Essence Kit for parents and their children. She also offers other essences for evolving consciousness.
http://www.angelicessences.com/index.htm

Daniel Mapel creates his **Wild Animal Essences** in a ceremonial process in the mountains of Virginia and I have yet to work with these fascinating essences. **Kat Bernard** gives testimonials to their effects.
http://www.animalessence.com/

Sage Holloway has written an incredible book called **Animal Healing and Vibrational Medicine** where she gives extensive information about all types of vibration healing Essences, of Flowers, Stars, Gems, Elements & Inert Gases, Environmental & Sacred Site Essences.
http://www.bluedolphinpublishing.com/Holloway.htm

Lila Devi developed **Masters Essences**, the second oldest Flower essence line, and wrote the book "**Flower Essences for Animals**." She describes working with aromatherapy in the East Indian context of using "**Koshas**" and with essences of **fruit trees** and **vegetables**.
http://www.mastersessences.com/Pets.html

Michele Small Wright's Perelandra Essences: **http://www.perelandra-ltd.com/**

Australian Bush Flower Essences **http://www.ausflowers.com.au/**

Alaskan Flower Essences **http://www.alaskanessences.com/**

Bailey Flower Essences **http://www.baileyessences.com/**

Findhorne Flower Essences **http://www.findhornessences.com/**

There are many others worldwide on the web.

Essences
by Alicia Rocco, NHP

Essences were founded by Dr. Edward Bach in the early 1900's and have been used extensively for emotional and spiritual healing. The essences are a tool for everyone to use not only for their animals but for the humans that share life with them.

Essences are subtle liquid extracts that can be used orally, in bath water, or as a spray mist. They are safe to use with food, medications, and any supplements because they work on the energetic level which in turn may affect the physical.

When communicating with animals the manner by which we receive the information is through the spirit of their emotions. I have been working with tree essences for a number of years and have found them to be the most effective tool to even enhance the communication as well as for the healing of the animal.

We offer 3 Canadian Forest Tree Essences that have been especially formulated for animals, as well as 12 Body Synergies for each system of the body.

Animal Rescue *– to be used for behavioral problems*
Animal Restore *– to restore the spirit of the animal due to trauma*
Animal Whisper *– for the animal that is aging and or may be dying*
12 Body Synergies *for each system of the body that may be in distress.*

Our office mascot, a miniature daschund was very distressed because I had to leave on a trip. He seemed to know when I made the plane reservation. Imagine that! He would not leave his bed or eat and was shaking. Using Animal Rescue and Animal Restore helped him to be able to function by allowing his system to respond in a calm manner and release his fear of abandonment. As a matter of fact I also took the essence because I felt guilty for leaving and knew that it would help me as well.

This same daschund had to have 3 hernia operations and each time I used essences before and after the surgery. Our vet relayed to us how he could not believe the disposition of the animal during the whole process. And everyone knows some daschunds can be snippy at times.

Recently we had a cat that our client was doctoring for constant urinary problems. When I first introduced the essence Urinary from our Body Synergy line to the owner she said she could not understand how the feelings of guilt could be related to the problems her cat was having. We discovered during the animal communication that the cat was taking on the owner's feelings of guilt and self esteem. Upon using the essence the urinary infection cleared up and did not return. Our animals will take on our hurts because of their love for us, therefore the cat wanted the owner to heal these emotional wounds. So needless to say the owner is taking Urinary as well.

A recent owner of a horse called to tell me she was having skittish problems with her horse that she had not experienced before. I suggested using Animal Whisper because of the aging of the horse and also Animal Rescue for the behavior. The horse had not been around children a great deal and the owner's grandchildren had moved in so when doing animal communication the horse explained it did not like the children and resented them being there. All of them have adjusted quite well but of course this was after both horse and children have taken essences.

Recently we had an animal that had cancer and was dying. We gave Animal Whisper to both animal and owner. The transition for the animal was more beautiful then words can say. The owner still continues the essences until the grieving process is completed.

Animals are very sensitive to the essence and I feel they respond even better than humans. I have noticed that if there is an issue the animal can use an essence and let go and move on where many times humans need to use them longer due to repeated cellular memory.

I have been an essence practitioner for over 15 years and have seen astounding healings.

*Our unique line of Tree Essences diluted in ready to use 1-oz. bottles may be purchased retail by going to our website at **www.naturalapproachtohealth.com** or by calling **330-868-4988** in the U.S.*

*We offer wholesale pricing as well as displays for Practitioner use. If you would like more training in the therapeutic use of our line of 3 animal, 12 body synergies, 7 single, and 16 combination tree essences, please see our web site for course schedules and self-study offerings, or contact me with questions via email at **alicia@naturalapproachtohealth.com***

Georgina's Note on the CFTE Essences. I often recommend one or more of the 38 Canadian Forest Tree Essences formulated for humans. In my experience, they work in exactly the same way for the animal as they would for a human, because the animals living with us, in our environment often display the same emotional challenges as we do.

How Essences are made

Dr. Bach's method of preparing the essences was to place the flowers in a clean clear bowl of distilled water and put the bowl in the sun for 3 hours. After 3 hours, the energetic transference of the "blueprint" or **vibrational resonance** of the flowers had occurred. The "source material," whether a flower, plant, tree, gem or any other substance, is then removed with only the energetic vibration of the substance remaining. The water is added to bottles half filled with brandy, then sealed and labeled. These are the **"mother" tinctures**, from which 2 drops are taken and put into the actual essence bottles along with distilled water.

Bach also used a **boiling method** for certain flowers if there was no sun and then made the "mother" tincture in the same way.

Making your own Essences

Essences can also be made by **using moonlight instead of the sun** and therefore the transference can be either "solar" or "lunar."

Dr. Masaru Emoto has photographed the **effects of thoughts on water** and taken pictures of the water before and after certain thoughts and this shows that **water will hold the resonance of anything put into it**, whether "real" or energetic.

I urge you to check out his website (link below) to really begin to understand how **our thoughts create the energy around us**, and how the water is showing us how thoughts, vibrations, frequencies and energies **imprint into reality and create the world**… and especially the water in us and around us.

http://www.life-enthusiast.com/twilight/research_emoto.htm

The **healing principle** of the essences is that an energy vibrating with a certain frequency may be used for the frequency it carries, to **balance or restore** what is missing in another's energetic vibrational frequency.

How to Make Gemstone Essences

The effect of a gemstone essence is based on **transference of the stone's energetic vibrational imprint** into the liquid.

The **best time to make a gemstone essence** is first thing in the morning when the moon is waxing, **past the first quarter** if possible, on a sunny day.

Place the stone in a **clear quartz crystal container** along with **distilled water**.

In the evening, move the container where it can be in the **moonlight** until the next morning.

The next morning, transfer the **energized water** (source removed) to a **dark-colored glass container**, seal and label. This is the treatment bottle

Store the treatment bottles in a dark area where they will not be exposed to extreme heat or light.

How Essences work

There are certain vibrational patterns that indicate a **disruption** in the pattern of a healthy body, allowing it to be "unhealthy" or to be vibrating in an irregular pattern. The vibrational remedies balance the subtle energies of the body by matching natural remedies to restore the pattern or health. When you take a particular vibrational pattern into your body, it continues to vibrate in its pattern, thus **synchronizing the other cells**, causing them to vibrate at that frequency. The **subtle essence vibration** affects the emotions in particular.

Essences help in a **gentle, non-invasive way** of assisting the animal on an emotional, spiritual level. In doing so, they help release blocks or irregular energy patterns to allow the body to heal in whatever way it can.

Animals spiritually allow the essences to work with them because they recognize the subtle yet **incredibly powerful assistance** an essence can provide for them. The essences help them to relax and be able to **release their emotions**, such as anger, fear, mistrust, anxiety etc.

Methods of Use

Ask permission of the animal first

Since animals who live in close quarters with humans often **share the same "energetic" influences,** be they emotional, physical or spiritual. It would be a wise thing for the human to also **take the same essences the animal is taking** ☺

Drops can be put into their **drinking water**, on the **ear tips**, inside the **mouth**, on the **paw pads** or sprayed onto the **fur or skin**.

Bach Flower and other Concentrated Essences

Bach Flower Essences, Anaflora Essences and some others are concentrated and must be diluted before use. For most **Bach Flower Essences**, a **basic dose** is **2-4 drops 2-3 times daily** or a **full dropperful** in the water bowl daily.

To make up a treatment bottle, choose the essence or essences to be used for treatment.

Fill a **clean, glass, one-ounce dropper bottle** ¾ full of purified spring water.

Add **2-4 drops of one essence** or if using more than one, **2 drops of each**.

Add 1 tablespoon of **brandy** to the bottle.

After filling and putting the stopper on, **tap the bottom of the bottle** to potentize it. This is the dosage bottle that you will use to give to your animal friend.

If there are concerns over using the brandy because of the alcohol content, please look into the various essence producers' explanations on it.
There are various reasons, but in general the essences do not seem to work the same with glycerin.

Also the doses are diluted and so **the alcohol content is so minute** that there is **less than 1 drop of alcohol in the actual dose**. There is more alcohol in ripe fruit. If using the essences externally, the alcohol will evaporate before the animal could absorb it.

Ready-to-Use Essences
Some essences are not concentrated. **Canadian Forest Tree Essences** are used directly out of the purchased bottle. They suggest 2-4 drops for small animals, 5-7 drops for dogs, horses, and humans.
Each essence company will have its own instructions for use, so always be sure to **read and follow the directions** on the labels.

Essence Chart – What to Use When

I have suggested below only the types of essences I have worked with, because I have not had a chance to try them all ☺. As there are so many… visit some of the recommended websites and feel what resonates with you as the types you would like to use for your animal friends.

Challenge	Bach Flower Essences	Canadian Forest Tree Essences	Anaflora Essences
Abandonment	Heather Chicory Cherry plum	Children's happy helping potion	Missing You
Abuse	Larch Dogwood Sweet Chestnut	Animal Restore	Return to Joy
Aggressiveness	Beech Holly Vine	Black Spruce	Aggression
Aging		Animal Whisper	Senior
Alpha challenging	Vine		
Anger	Beech Holly Vine	Black spruce	Aggression
Anxiety	Aspen Cerato Mimulus	Milennium Journey	Special stress
Attention	Clematis Heather Impatiens	Forest secrets	Good dog
Brokenheartedness	Honeysuckle Sweet chestnut Gorse	Animal restore	Return to joy Pound puppies and kittens
Calming	Star of Bethlehem Rock rose White chestnut Rescue remedy	Animal rescue Yellow birch	Tranquility
Change	Walnut		
Confidence	Elm Larch Mimulus	Ponderosa pine	Good dog

Challenge	Bach Flower Essences	Canadian Forest Tree Essences	Anaflora Essences
	Centauri		
Death & dying	Star of Bethlehem Wild rose	Animal whisper	Bereavement
Defensiveness	Agrimony Beech Holly Red chestnut Willow	Rocky mountain juniper Western hemlock	
Denial	Agrimony Willow	Western hemlock	
Depression	Mustard Elm Gentian Gorse Wild rose	Red alder	Loneliness
Destructiveness	Cherry plum Holly	Black spruce	Aggression
Discouragement	Gentian Gorse Wild rose	Red alder	Feral cat comforter
Dislike	Beech Holly	Black spruce	Aggression
Dominance	Vine	Black spruce	
Eating disorders	Cherry plum Gentian	Body image & weight control	
Erratic behavior	Cherry plum Agrimony Rock rose Scleranthus	Forest secrets	
Exhaustion or fatigue	Elm Hornbeam Oak Olive	Animal restore	Recovery remedy
Failure	Centauri Chestnut bud Elm Larch Oak	Ponderosa pine	

Challenge	Bach Flower Essences	Canadian Forest Tree Essences	Anaflora Essences
Fear	Aspen Mimulus Rock rose	Millennium journey	Special stress
Flexibility	Oak Rock water Walnut Pussy willow		New beginnings
Frustration	Beech Impatiens	Rocky mountain juniper	
Grief	Star of Bethlehem Wild rose	Animal restore	Bereavement
Groundedness	Cherry plum Clematis Scleranthus Star of Bethlehem Vervain	Yellow birch	Tranquility
Guilt	Elm Pine	Family relations	Return to joy
Healing	Crabapple Hornbeam Olive	Animal restore	Post surgery
Inadequacy/jealousy	Agrimony Centauri Cerato Larch Vine	Life embrace	Tranquility
Insecurity	Agrimony Aspen Centauri Cerato Chicory Larch	Life embrace	Tranquility
Learning difficulties	Chestnut bud Wild oak	Life embrace	Good dog
Loneliness	Elm Heather Honeysuckle	Life embrace	Loneliness Return to joy

Challenge	Bach Flower Essences	Canadian Forest Tree Essences	Anaflora Essences
	Mustard		
Obsession	Agrimony Cherry plum Chicory Heather Sweet chestnut Vervain White chestnut	Yellow birch	Tranquility
Overprotectiveness	Chicory Red chestnut	Black spruce	
Overwhelmed	Aspen Elm Star of Bethlehem Sweet chestnut	Forest secrets	tranquility
Panic	Aspen Rock rose Star of Bethlehem	Millennium journey	Tranquility
Resentment	Beech Vine Willow	Western hemlock	Aggression
Resignation	Centauri Gentian Gorse Mustard Wild rose	Red alder	Bereavement
Resistance	Beech Cerato Chestnut bud Willow	Western hemlock	Harmony
Restlessness	Impatiens White chestnut	Yellow birch	Tranquility
Security	Cerato Honeysuckle	Animal rescue	Recovery remedy Special stress
Selfishness	Chicory Water violet Holly Willow	Family relations	Harmony

Challenge	Bach Flower Essences	Canadian Forest Tree Essences	Anaflora Essences
Shock	Star of Bethlehem Rescue remedy	Animal rescue	Recovery remedy
Stoic	Agrimony	Red alder	Return to joy
Strength	Centauri Hornbeam Oak Olive	Therapist & healer	New beginnings
Tolerance	Agrimony Beech Rock water Vervain Vine Willow	Pussy willow	Tranquility
Transition	Honeysuckle Walnut	Animal restore	Relocation
Trauma	Aspen Star of Bethlehem Rescue remedy	Animal rescue	Recovery remedy
Trust	Aspen Cerato Larch Mimulus	Ponderosa pine	Feral cat comforter
Victim consciousness	Agrimony Aspen Centauri	Ponderosa pine	Feral cat comforter

Canadian Forest Tree Essences has many other essences and combinations. They also have a full line of essences for body systems of the animals.

There are **12 Body Synergy Essences** for: Digestive System, Intestinal System, Glandular System, Nervous System, Respiratory System, Urinary System, Circulatory System, Immune System, Reproductive System, Structural (Bones) System, Muscles and Skin.

AnaFlora Essences make special "**higher consciousness**" blends and special needs blends. They also make individual essences, as well as custom blend essences specifically for your animal, as well as yourself.

There are many other wonderful producers of Essences. I just have not had a chance to try them all out yet.

There are also Angel Essences, Animal Spirit Essences, Crystal Essences, Shell Essences, Gem Essences and Elixirs, Starlight Essences & Elixirs, Elements and Inert Gas Essences, Environmental and Sacred Site Essences.

Essences can be made of up just about anything. When you have some free time, try some searches on Google to see what is available on the Internet.

Essence Practice Exercises

Learn about the Essences Intuitively

Step 1. Breathing
Using the breath is vitally important to any type of physical healing or energy healing work. The breath gives us life, and also connects us to all things. When we learn how to breathe properly, we enable ourselves to experience better health. We are also able to become more aware of everything around us, simply by breathing.
Breathing properly and deeply, physically improves our circulation, which brings oxygen to all of our organs and facilitates the body's proper functioning.

Place your hand on your abdomen, and with your abdominal muscles, push your hand out. Feel how that action automatically draws in your breath. That is how deeply you should be breathing.

Fill Your Lungs all the way to the Bottom

Shallow breathing merely brings the air into your upper lungs. You want to completely fill your lungs all the way to the bottom.

When you inhale, do so slowly and to the count of five. When you get to five, hold your breath for 2 seconds. Then begin to exhale, also to the count of five.

Step 2.

Find a comfortable place to sit or lie down and place one hand on your abdomen.

Take a deep breath, preferably through your nose. You may breathe through your mouth only if breathing through your nose is uncomfortable.

Draw your breath in deeply, into the bases of your lungs until you feel your abdomen rise and you reach the count of five.

Hold your breath for 2 seconds.

Gently exhale and release your breath, preferably through your nose. Exhale through your mouth only if breathing through your nose is uncomfortable. As you exhale, you will feel the hand on your abdomen go down. Exhale to the count of five.

Repeat…

After you have practiced this a few times, you can put your hands comfortably wherever you like, so that your body feels totally relaxed.

Go into your heart space by breathing.

Breathe deeply and go into your space. Visualize the essence that you wish to connect with.

Imagine the smell of the essence.

Continue breathing deeply and allow yourself to blend into the energy of the essence. Ask the essence to share with you what its qualities are and what it would like to teach you.

Write down everything that you have experienced about the essence.

Choose 1 essence a week to work with. Tune into it at least three times during the week to see how the information shifts or changes depending on your own vibrational changes during the week.

Exercise 1

Assessing the Effect of an Essence on an Animal

Go into your space by using the above White Light Technique or the one you learned in Georgina's Animal Communication Course "module 1", or any other meditative techniques where you work from the Heart for the Highest Good of All.

Breathe into your space. Tune into your pet or the pet you are working on.

Sense the **feelings** that you are working to try to help with. Get a sense of evaluating how they feel.

After you have tuned into the animal, choose the appropriate essence.

Use the essence with the animal in one of the methods described earlier in this section. Wait 10 minutes.

Gently and respectfully **tune into the animal again**. Sense the **difference** that the animal feels after the essence. You can use this method to evaluate the effects of the essence and how much or how little to use. Be sure to **record the effects and changes** for each animal.

Exercise 2

Getting to know the Bach Flower Essences.
Go into your space by using the White Light Technique.

Breathe into your Heart space. Tune into the essence. Ask the essence to share the experience of being "it." Ask it if it has any messages for you.

Become familiar with each essence in this way. Get to know them. You can then ask them to guide you in how to use them.

Be sure to **journal** the information you receive.

Exercise 3

Getting to know the Tree Essences

If at all possible **go outside and lie on the ground** to do the meditation and getting into your space. Go into your space by using the White Light Technique going into your heart Space.

Place about **7 to 10 drops** of the tree essence of your choice onto your **tongue**.

Allow your senses to open and become aware as you begin your deep breathing. **Imagine the tree that you are connecting with**, tasting and tuning into.

Feel yourself energetically **merging with the energy of the tree**. Allow yourself to **open and receive the information** that the tree has to share with you.

Evaluate your feelings and **how they shift** as you are one with the tree.

Gently **bring your awareness back** to the present and **write down your experience** in detail.

Exercise 4

Getting to know Anaflora Essences.
Choose Sharon Callahan's **Expanded States Essence**. Before communicating with one of your pets, **both of you take the essence**.

Go into your heart space and tune into your animal friend. This essence is specifically to help you to **achieve a deeper awareness** in you and your animal friends meditation together.

Exercise 5

Getting to know the Shamanic Animal Essences.
Choose one of Ruth Joy's **Shamanic Animal Essences**, go into your space, tune into the animal of that essence. Ask the animal whose essence you are tuned into **what you need to know about the essence** and how you should work with it.

Do this with as many of the Shamanic Animal Essences possible, getting to know each one.

Keep a journal of your findings.

Exercise 6

Getting to know the Angelic Essences
Practice getting to know the Angelic Essences in Ruth Joys **Angelic Spiritual Growth Awakening Essences**. There are ones for Attunement, Coming Home, Connecting to Source, Manifestation, DNA connecting and others that are wonderful to meditate with and experience. **Choose one, go into your space** and don't forget to **write down your experience in detail**.

PART IV: CONCLUSION

For thousands of years, all cultures have had a history of having "medicine People" working to help with illness and health problems of all kinds. The "cures" were searched out through various healing experiments, which included physical and energetic treatments and remedies--from foods, to herbs, to poisons.

"Prescriptions" have been found carved into clay tablets in the Egyptian times. Medical advancements within the last 100 years has taken us into the world of pharmaceuticals (which are mostly derived from herbs or created synthetically) and surgical procedures as well as advanced treatments that have changed and saved countless lives.

There is a need for *both* today's conventional medicine and the age old traditional alternative therapies. I would like to see the two combined, or at least working together as complementary medicine.

Regarding conventional medicine, I suggest that you research and take courses to learn about conventional medicine, how most veterinarians work with it, and how you can assist them in what they do.

Regarding alternative therapies, there are literally thousands of "natural" traditional remedies that have been used since humans appeared on earth. These remedies vary with cultures around the world.

African Priests are regarded as gods once they have demonstrated their omnipotence by handling burning embers, and using native plants and herbs.

Ayurvedic methods may utilize steam-filled sweat boxes, meditation, as well as diet, sleep modification, yoga, herbs and cleansing.

The **Native American Shaman** may use the sweat lodge, the rhythm of drums, the pain of ordeal, and arrows of the magic plants as well as herbs such as sage inhaled and brushed around the body.

In **Pakistan, a century-old** tradition is to use a paste of hazelnut powder and oils, known as surma, which is spread in and around the eyes of the children to protect them from illness.

In **Swaziland, a healer** called a Sangoma will "read" an assortment of objects thrown on a mat similar to "runes" to receive the information that is needed to help the patient.

The **Tibetan** healers may use the transformation of tantric deities influencing the passage of time, astrological charts, and methods such as moxa bustion and pulse taking.

The body's own innate ability to heal is demonstrated when the immune system eats up viruses and bacteria on its own, when collagen develops to heal a wound…wonders that science may assist, but cannot yet reproduce.

Any instinctual touch with thoughts of love and healing come from the white light of love and the white light of love has the highest power to heal so that is the biggest gift you can give.

I hope you have enjoyed this Essence Ebook

Light Blessings,

Georgina Cyr

Made in the USA
Coppell, TX
31 January 2022

72713613R00015